Ear of the Spirit

Proverbs 27:17

J C BEAVER

J C Beaver

"He that an ear, let him hear what the Spirit,"

saith unto the churches;

Revelation 2:7

Paula & David,

I pray the two of you enjoy this book. You may learn something about me you don't know.

Wahooooo!

Love ya'll, Joyce

All rights reserved. No part of this publication may be reproduced, stored in a retrieval system, transmitted in any form or by any means, electronic, mechanical, photocopy, recording, or by any other means without prior permission from publisher.

Copyright @ 2014   J C BEAVER

All rights reserved

ISBN: 13:978-1500867325

ISBN: 10:1500857327

CONTENTS

This book is laid out for you to read in sections, not chapters. When you read a sections, and think you understand it, ask yourself this question.

Am I willing to abide by the word of God when I read it? If you answer, "I don't know," go back, re-read what you just read.

This book is written to write in. Get a red pen, yellow pen, green pen. When you read something that sounds weird to you, mark it in read. Then go look it up in the Word of God. When you read something that makes you say, "Oh, yes!" Mark it in green. That pleases the Lord. When you read something you absolutely do not understand, mark it in yellow, and research it until you do understand. IF NO UNDERSTANDING COMES, PRAY AND ASK GOD FOR WISDOM. HE IS THE WISDOM GIVER.

All of the stories are true. They are not parables. Only one was told to me, the rest are first-hand knowledge.

ACKNOWLEDGMENTS

Several people brought this book to bear: Thank you:

I would like to say to Mrs. Pearl Gillenwater. You have been such an inspiration to me. All the wonderful discussions, we have had about the Lord and His wonderful work, your kindness and care toward me and my family.

To Deloris George who bought the first book I ever wrote.

To Chris Hornback. You help me through the process, you encouraged me, when I wanted to give up, and you made me do it, when I didn't understand what I was doing.

To Martha Patterson. My lifelong friend, sister*n*law, confidant, devil stomping prayer-buddy, and helper in stamping out the path we have been taking together, since we were in high school...Thank you for sticking closer than a brother when I fell off the wagon and got lost for a couple of years.

To my sister Janice Edins. Thank you for helping me edit these books. We stayed up many night, and let the battery in our phones go out, but we got it done.

Thanks to all my family and friends who take the time to read my books. Also, thanks for telling me where to find and fix the errors. I do love you. Jesus loves you.

DEDICATION

I dedicate this book to anyone and everyone who will take the initiative and begin to seek the

LORD

With all their heart, mind, soul, will, emotions'.

My prayer with you is:

"Into your hands Lord do I come, all of me for all of You!"

Ear of the Spirit

Are you an inquisitive person? We should be inquisitive people. We should ask questions of people, and the Lord. I ask questions of the Lord most people don't even think about. I want to know the truth. I want to be set free from all things that are displeasing to the Lord. I want my soul and body to line up with the Word, the Spirit, and the image of the Lord.

Are you a friendly person? We should be friendly people who loves people, good, bad and ugly. I want everyone to know the Lord, who loves them; the good, the bad and the ugly ones. Do you remember being one of the good, bad, uglies before you got saved? I do. I remember how I didn't want to talk to people, or be around them whether they knew the Lord or not. People are not as nice as dogs. Dogs love you unconditionally. People haven't learned to do that, not even a lot of the saved ones.

Are you a person who likes to be told the truth? We should be people who likes to be *told* the truth, even if it hurts. I have a tendency to do that to people, who don't want to hear it. But God wants us to tell it and to hear it. I believe, if you want a serious relationship with Father, it is time you get serious. It is time to hear the truth and do it.

Are you radical, fanatical, or relational? Some people want to call me a radical Christian or even a fanatic. I looked up both those words, and found out, I really didn't know the meaning of either one. I know the ones who want to call me such, don't know the meaning of the words. You probably don't either. So let us be enlighten by what we find.

Radical means, arising from, or going to, a root or source, fundamental, basic. Favoring or designating a word root. (Then there are the other meanings that deal with the political side of the word - since I am not a political person, we won't go there)

Fanatic means: A person possessed by an excessive and irrational zeal, especially for a religion or political cause.

Relationship is another word that makes people weird. You think you know the meaning of that one?

Let me ask you a question right here. Did you really know what any of those words mean? Do you understand there is a difference between these words? If you could write out what you believe about these words; would you say, I am one of those words, I am none of those words? This is where we all need to go and ask ourselves, "am I willing to become more than I am?"

This is where I am on this subject, because I want the ear of the Spirit to operate in me every minute of every day, so I can hear the Holy Spirit speak to me every day, not just on Sunday morning in a building where I go to meet and hear preaching. If I am only hearing the Spirit speak to me through preaching on Sunday morning, I am not listening to the Lord. Do you think He only talks through a preacher?

I think, we, as Christian's are not thinking about what we are reading, when we read the Word. The Word should be speaking to us every time we read a scripture, a verse, and a book of the Bible. Because there is a deeper place we can go with the Spirit of the Lord. We can hear Him, if we are listening, while driving the car, walking to the grocery store, going to the movies, fishing at the lake, hunting in the woods, working at our desk during the day. We can hear Him speak to us anywhere, at any time, if we are listening with the ear of the Spirit.

What does it mean to hear?

_____

_____

What does it mean to listen?

_____

_____

Bible Importance

     Someone told me they had never heard the Spirit speak to them. In listening to the conversation, I realized they did not understand what hearing consist of. I asked, "Do you read your Bible?" "Yes, but I never hear anything. I don't even understand the words I am reading," came the answer in quick response. "How long have you been a Christian?" I asked. "I was born in the church. All my family and I have attended church, all my life. I was raised in a religious home, and all my family are Christians." they said. I listened to them and asked the Lord, "What is wrong with this conversation?" Here is someone who was raised in Church, whose entire family go every time the doors are open, and they believe they are a Christian, because they were raised, as a Christian. If they had been listening with the ear of the Spirit, they would know, 'ye must be born again, or ye cannot see the kingdom of God.' This does not say, 'they cannot go to the kingdom of God', it says, 'he cannot see the kingdom of God.' Here is a young person, who has been raised in church, gone to Sunday school since they came out of nursery, been in revivals, reads the bible, hears the preaching every Sunday, and is not saved. How do we know that? They do not confess they are born again, because they doesn't know what born again means. They think they are a Christian, because they go to Church, lives in a Christian family, reads the bible, and keeps the law (doesn't do bad stuff). I am not judging this young person, just stating the facts. They need to be born again, so they can *see and hear* the Spirit of the Lord, speak to them, and understand what they are reading. The kingdom of God is within you, so says the Word. (Luke 17:21) If the kingdom is not within you, you cannot hear the Spirit speaking to you.

Listening is as important as hearing.

A lady and I got into a conversation about hearing the Spirit speak to us. She related a story to me, and I shook my head in sadness.

So many people in the building, they are calling a church have missed the boat, and don't even know it. The Bible is not a bunch of stories, written down to entertain you, it is not a myth, not a history book, even though it is a book of Bible history.

The Bible is the express image of God, working in the lives of mankind, down the portals of time, till Jesus was born. Then it becomes the human expression of God in Flesh, demonstrating the life, he planned for man to live. He then leads us into what He expects of us with our fellowman, and how to live with one another in the abundance, He laid out for us to live on earth. He ends the book telling us what will happen in the last days, due to man's inability to live the life He set down for us to live. We entertain evil, calling it good, allowing the enemy to destroy the good life He created for His free children. Bondage is what the evil one wants to place upon the race, and bondage is what is out there facing the entire race, who wants to follow the prince of the power of the air.

"Wow," you are saying. "This is deep." No, this is life. Deep is when the water is over your head, you can't breathe, because you are standing on the bottom. Let's examine what the scripture says about hearing.

The Lord gave me the scriptures in the order they are listed. He will explain them.

Hearing – Romans 10:17 - so then faith comes by hearing, and hearing by the word of God.

Hearing faith comes by hearing the Word of God. There are many ways to hear the Word, you can read it out loud to yourself, or you can listen to CD's of someone else reading to you. You can listen to the preaching of sermon's on Sunday morning, watch preachers on TV, and go to bible studies. There are endless ways to hear the Word and receive faith. But you have to make the time, take the time, and put an effort into listening to the word. You can hear, yet not listen to what the Spirit is saying. As you hear the Word, listen for the Holy Spirit to interpret the Word to your spirit. Don't just hear, listen to the Spirit. If you aren't praying, asking the Spirit to give you understanding, or it won't matter what you hear.

Acts 28:26 - go you unto the people, and say, hearing ye shall hear, and shall not understand; and seeing you shall see, and not perceive.

There are going to be people, who will hear and not understand, they will see and not perceive. Why does this happen? Let's read the next verse. *For the heart of this people is waxed gross*, (lacking sensitivity or discernment, carnal, dense, thick, and overweight, exclusive of deduction.) In other words, their *heart* is not right with the Lord. They don't have a relationship, they have a religion. Did you know, if you only have religion instead of relationship, you will maintain your own idea of what you believe, by what you decide is right or wrong. God's Word is specific on what is right, what is wrong.

He speaks to you and you obey. Obedience is loving God enough to obey in all things whether you like it or not. If you don't like it, it does not matter, He is always right and you are the one who has to line up with the Word of God. You want to know why so many people are overweight. They over eat. In other words, they are gluttons. The Word tells us not to be gluttons, but do we hear, do we listen? No, we eat what we want too, when we want too, and as much as we want too. We are overweight, because we don't hear the Word of God, we don't listen to what God tells us. We deceive ourselves into believing what we are doing is what God wants us to be doing. If we were actually listening and hearing the Spirit, we would not be over eating or over weight. We would be obedient to the Word in all things. Oh, but I am learning, some may say. How long does it take us to read, hear the Spirit and obey? I know this, how? Keep reading.

Amos 8:11 - behold, the days come, saith the Lord God, that I will send a <u>famine in the land,</u> not a famine of bread, nor a thirst for water, but a <u>hearing of the words</u> of the Lord.

The Lord is *sending* a *famine* in the *land.* Look at the list: not a *famine* of *bread,* (*food.*) Nor a thirst for water, so food and water will still be available to those who want it. The Lord is sending a famine of the hearing of the words of the Lord. Another way of saying, He won't make it plain to the people, He won't open their eyes to see or their ears to hear. I wondered why He would do that and it came to me. People are more *interested* in fulfilling self-interest than obeying God. The Lord knows if you are seriously obeying or going to obey. He knows everything you think, feel, and say before you do it. He wants us to wake up and hear Him and obey. This is what it means to die to self. As long as self is in charge, we are deceiving ourselves. Obedience is better than sacrifice. The world has their attention held by games on the I-pad, computer games, movies, television, *and weekends* in the mountains, weekends fishing, hunting, weekends of vacation taken at the casino, *running* to and fro, and chasing the everlasting work schedule that could be called the never ending story.

Self-interest, is what 'I' want, when 'I' want it and as much as 'I' want. If it is all about 'I', it is really, all about self. How can we know if it is 'I'? Are you over-indulging the flesh? If you are, it is still about 'I'. God's people have to make a choice to obey God. Right means right. Eat right, talk right, and love right, live obedient (right).

Someone said, 'give us an example of what it means being about 'I'.

Example: How tall are you? _____.

You should weigh one hundred pounds for the first five feet and five lbs. for each inch over five feet. Calculate that. If you are over the amount of weight you are supposed to be, you are indulging the flesh and it is still all about self.

Matt 13:13 - Therefore speak I to them in parables; because they seeing, see not; and hearing, they hear not, neither do they understand.

The Lord speaks to the people in parables. He knows the people will not see, because they believe they are seeing and hearing, but actually they are so busy with the worldly things, they don't have time to actually see what the Lord is doing right in front of them. Their plan is better in their eyes than what the Lord is doing, because He isn't moving as fast as they want Him too. The reason they don't understand is, they don't know, nor do they read their bible, God's word. People are self-aggrandizing with no thought about what the Lord wants. Some even think they are doing what the Lord wants, because they are religious in their heart and mind. Aren't we supposed to be religious? Let's look up the word.

Religious: Of or pertaining to religion or teaching religion. Adhering to or manifesting religion; pious.

These terms have in common, a mental, emotional or reverential attitude about religion. Religion implies, adherence to religion in both belief, and practice. Religious devotion to duty.

A religious person will go to church every time the doors are open, take their kids with their I-phone, I-pods or hand held computers allowing their children to play games during the service. I have seen adults and teens doing the same things. I witnessed a deacon of the church playing a game with his I-phone several Sunday mornings. I have seen teens doing their homework while services are going on, young marrieds TX-messaging one another across the room. This ought not to be. Religion is ok with whatever. Religion has its own idea of what worship is, and does not do much with worship. There are hardly any salvations in the services today. The same four people go down to the front every service asking prayer for the same things over and over, getting no answers. I have sat in church and seen people walking in and out all during the service. Children running in and out during the service, and lots of kids playing games on their phones. Parents don't care or don't see what is going on. There is no discipline where the kids are concerned, or the adults for that matter. But, we are supposed to be religious, you say. Are we supposed to be religious, or are we supposed to be in a relationship, with the Lord Jesus Christ?

Let's look at the word relationship. When you have relationship, you are connected to that person, you are one with them. Just like the Word says, we are supposed to be one with Jesus, which makes us. One with the Father.

Relationship: the condition or fact of being related. Connection by blood or marriage, kinship.

Where are you, where am I, in the view God wants His people to have? Ask yourself this question,

Am I religious or am I in relationship with Jesus?

Tired

One morning, when I woke up at two a.m., my mind was tired, my body was tired. I had not slept much when I went to bed, due to the things going on in our family that I had been praying about. Rebuking sickness, my flesh was taking an upper respiratory infection from the junk in the air. Two a.m. seemed like an hour from hell, the way I felt. I had only been in bed three hours, if that. I wanted to go back to sleep. I prayed, "Lord, give me another couple of hours sleep."

I heard a cry from the other room, the baby was awake and crying. My mind must have anticipated her waking up. I could not ignore that cry, but my mind wanted too. My body wanted to turn over, pull the covers over my head and ignore the cry.

The Lord spoke to my heart. "You can do all things, for I strengthen you." I felt a sudden rush of joy in my Spirit, as I smiled turning over, to get out of bed, walking quickly to the cry. I prayed, "Thank you, Father, for Jesus who is the joy of my strength. Thank you for peace, and thank you for extra faith to believe, you are more than able to do in me what your Word says."

When I got to the baby, I realized why she was crying with such noise. She had poop running all over herself and her bed. She wanted cleaned up. I shook my head, as I picked Precious up, began cleaning her and the mess up. The Lord reminded me, "I have cleaned up your messes more than once. No one likes laying in the pig-pen slop, especially when you are too young to know what it is. You are called, you are chosen to be my hands to care for, and clean up after babies everywhere, and who will have ears to hear."

As I finished cleaning up, I dropped the mess from the clean-up rag. Baby-girl quickly slapped at it, moved to touch it, then realized it smelled bad. She moved away from it, looking at me, as if to say, "What is that stinking stuff?" I smiled, as I picked up the messy yuck, taking everything to the trashcan. I wasn't going to wash anything, just throw it all away, and start fresh. With everything cleaned up, baby was bathed from head to toe in warm cleansing water, and baby powder smelling shampoo. As I lay her down, patted her, I said quietly too her drowsy self, "Jesus loves you, I love you, and you are clean by the grace of God."

I felt the presence of the Lord, as I realized what I had just spoken, was true of me too. He had found me years ago, crying in the mess I had made of my life. He came to me, picked me up out of it, cleaned me and began teaching me who He was for me, to me and in me. He was for me, not against me. He had died on the cross for my sins (mess). When He asked me to believe, I chose to believe, He took it from there. He forgave me, washed me in His blood, and has taught me from that day to this, He is who He says He is, and I am His treasure.

Baby girl is a treasure to me, and I am a treasure to Him! When I obey, things go His way. Good!

It is Written

Mark 6:2 - and when the Sabbath day was come, He began to teach in the synagogue; and many hearing him were astonished, saying, from whence hath this man these things? And what wisdom is this which is given unto him, that even such mighty works are wrought by his hands? Is not this the carpenter; the son of Mary, the brother of James and Jose, and of Juda and Simon? And are not his sisters here with us. And they were offended at him.

This scripture says, 'when the Sabbath day was come.' The Sabbath day is the day of rest. So, Jesus took this time of rest to teach in the synagogue. The synagogue is to the Jews, what the church is to the Christian. Today, many go to a building they call a church. They forget this building is just a building, they worship in. The church of Jesus Christ is you. You are the church. Jesus is the head, you are the body. Selah (stop and **Think about that.)**

He is in charge of His body, so if you are the church (body), He is in charge of you. He is responsible for your abundant life, He is responsible for your healing, your prosperity, your growth, your cleanliness, your well-being, everything in you, and He is responsible for teaching you how to live this life. So, what am I responsible for? As His body, His church-body, we are responsible to read His Word, learn who he is in us and obey what He tells us to do, when He tells us, do it. We are responsible for telling the truth, living the truth, and letting Him be leader in our lives. How often we fail, is determined by how often we obey. If we obey Him, we cannot fail. Why? Because it is not us doing the work. Father is doing it, as He was doing it through Jesus. Do you remember when Jesus said, "I and my Father are one?" (John 10:30) If Jesus and the Father are ONE, then if Jesus lives in us, we are one with Him also. Jesus said, 'He did nothing except what he saw the Father do.' Is that true in our lives? Jesus never failed at anything he saw the Father doing, then we should be in that place, if we are in obedience to his Word. If you are Jesus' sheep, then you should be believing Him and obeying Him.

A dietitian told me, "You are over-weight and you don't have to be." I wanted to say, "Really? Tell me why I don't have to be?" Before I could say what I was thinking, she preceded to say, "If you would obey, and eat properly, your body would lose that extra weight, without having to try. I want you to consider obeying, what is proper for your body." She gave me a carb schedule she said would work for me to lose weight. She told me, I should weigh 100 pounds for the first five feet of my height and 5 lbs. for each inch over five feet. So I calculated that to mean, I should weigh about 135 lbs. I was amazed that the reason I was at 199 lbs. was disobedience. That means I am disappointing my Father, because I am eating to satisfy my flesh. Being overweight was my fault, because I wasn't living up to my Father's word. I repented and asked Father to help me obey in this situation. Three weeks later, I had lost eight pounds. Father is faithful when we are in obedience. We can make excuses all day long, but in the end, we are the one responsible for whether we obey or disobey. Someone once told me, "I have a disorder that causes me to be overweight." I wanted to say, "Me too. It's caused disobedience."

GRACE

Act 5:5 - and Ananias hearing these words fell down, and gave up the ghost: and great fear came on all these that hear these words.

In the story of Ananias, we learn he and his wife lied to the Holy Ghost. When questioned by the disciple about what he and his wife were telling, he lied first to the disciples, in the Holy Ghost. When she was questioned, she lied to the disciples and Holy Ghost. They both fell down and died. If that happened today, most of the world would be lying dead in the streets. God's grace is keeping that from happening today. We should be thankful that we are living under the grace of God. I have heard preachers saying, some are preaching hyper-grace: meaning you can do whatever you want too, and still go to heaven. Others are not preaching grace, only the cross: meaning you come to the cross, accept Jesus and you are saved.

Grace in the Greek concordance means, unmerited favor, kindness, forgiveness. Every living soul is receiving a measure of grace, or none of us would not be alive. I believe God knows our frail flesh isn't able to understand, so He grants to all living things, a measure of grace, and a measure of faith. It is up to us to develop the measure given, and do something with it, so it will grow.

Grace is what you got, so you could come to the cross. God's grace is a free gift. He gives it to all. Not all, accept it. If you read the story of the one's given a pound, in Luke 19:12-27, and how the three used it, you will see a little of what grace is. Grace is God's divine love, and protection bestowed freely upon mankind, period. The bad, good and ugly, all are given grace by God. If you come to the cross, and believe what He says, about His son, then you are extended the grace of being forgiven, (to pardon, to excuse for a fault or offense,), and sanctified, (made holy) by the favor of God. We call it, being born again. If you begin to read, study, pray, obey, then you are extended more grace; an excellence or *power* granted by God; an *unmerited gift* from God. Some call it Holy Spirit baptism. God's calling is without repentance. When He calls, He empowers you to do whatever He calls you to do. He gives you grace to accomplish the task, if you love, obey Him and believe Him.

When He calls you, he will do in, and through you what he calls you to do. If you call yourself, you have no power from him, and will wear yourself out trying to do something for God, he is not even involved in. I have watched people struggle, thinking they are doing this wonderful thing for God, when it fails, they wonder why. When they get miserable in the doing, they blame God. It isn't his fault, you chose to get involved in a project He didn't call you too. They have not considered, God wasn't in it from the start. God isn't in all good works. Many works are the works of the flesh, and will be burned up in the last days. There are many wood, hay, and stubble events in our lives, we think are good works of God. Many will be surprised on the Day of Judgment to find most, if not all of their good works are burned up, because of the attitude in the doing.

Acts 18:8 And Crispus the chief ruler of the synagogue, believed on the Lord with his whole house, and many of the Corinthian's hearing believed and were baptized.

Here a CHIEF ruler of the synagogue believed on the Lord….. And his whole house…This was an enigma. A chief ruler could have been a Rabbi. This chief ruler believed on Jesus and his whole house got saved.

Nicodemus was another ruler in the temple. I have heard preachers preach that Nicodemus didn't actually accept Jesus when he met him on that night, the two got together to talk. My reading of that episode, finds no evidence of Jesus even asking him anything about what he believed. Jesus only taught him what it was he needed to do to be born-again. He left it strictly up to Nicodemus to make up his own mind, in his own time, decide if he really knew the scriptures, and did he want to know the savior? Grace allows you to make up your own mind, about what you want from the Lord. Just because you know the scriptures, does not mean you are going to heaven. Jesus made a point of telling Nicodemus, 'you must be born of the water and the spirit.' Why did he say water and spirit? What does it mean in scripture?

(4151=**spirit**- pneuma: to breathe hard, a rational soul, mental disposition, Christ's Spirit, the Holy Ghost.) The Word of God is meant by water here.

Ephesians 5:26 states, that he might sanctify, and cleanse it with the washing of water by the Word. Jesus was saying to Nicodemus, it was necessary for him to be born from above by the Spirit. Nicodemus knew he had been born of woman at one time, and he was thinking, Jesus meant he had to do it again. Jesus was telling him, it wasn't of the flesh, but of the Spirit, he must be born. Ask yourself, have you considered grace is sufficient for you to make the decision, on whether you want to go to heaven or not?

WOMAN

Jesus tells the woman at the well, whosoever drinks of this water shall thirst again, but whosoever drinks of the water that I shall give her shall never thirst; but the water Jesus gives shall spring up in you, as a well of water springing up into everlasting life. In *John 7:38, Jesus tells us, he that believes on him, as the scriptures has said, out of his belly shall flow rivers of living water.* When Jesus died on the cross, the soldier with a spear pierced his side, and forthwith came there out blood and water. When we draw near to Christ with a true heart in full assurance of faith, having our hearts sprinkled from an evil conscience and our bodies washed with pure water (Spirit), we have eternal life. My sister's five year old granddaughter, Katie, told her one evening, "Nana, Jesus washes you in the water of His Word, and cleanses you with His blood." Out of the mouth of a child, he shall lead them.

Heb 5:11- of whom we have many things to say, and hard to be uttered, seeing ye are dull of hearing.

The reason people fail to hear is, they become dull of hearing. It is easier to watch TV, listen to music on the radio, turn on your I-pod than it is to get into God's Word and read. Schools are not teaching children to read, and comprehend what they read. Common sense has been split with humming, or sitting cross-legged in a group, using a blank mind to communicate with the dead or demons. Yes, demons are real. They plague the saved, and unsaved. Strongholds keep Christians in bondage for years, because that demon that sits on your shoulder is there to convince you that you don't have any strongholds. You cannot concentrate on the Word when you read, because the enemy of your soul is your familiar spirit, sitting in your space to keep you distracted. You can't hear God speaking to you, your familiar spirit is talking too loud for you to distinguish between the two. I have heard people say, "Christians don't have demons." Call it whatever you want too, but a stronghold is actually demonic in nature. It means, an area of predominance. So anything that is keeping you from obeying God, is a stronghold, and has predominance in your life. You need deliverance from that stronghold, so you can hear and obey God.

The Challenge

God wants all to be saved. Will all be saved? There are ministries that teach all will be saved. I do not think this is scriptural. Did Judas get saved? Did the Pharisees get saved? Do you think everyone is going to heaven? Will the anti-Christ followers get saved? I believe when Jesus said, broad is the way that leads to destruction and narrow is the way to heaven, He meant not a lot of people are going to make it, because they don't like the narrow way that has been set down. Someone dear to me asked me this question, 'if God is real, why doesn't he just appear to me and show me?' I asked, "Do you mind if I pray for you to have a supra-natural encounter with the Lord?" "Go ahead, but I don't believe He will?" came the negative reply. All I could think of was, 'according to your faith, be it unto you.' Rationally speaking, that is the way most people live. "Go ahead, but I don't believe it.

Question:

1. Are you saved?_____
2. How do you know?
3. Do you know someone who needs salvation?
4. Write their names:

5. Pray this prayer for them: Lord, You have finished what is necessary for these folks and me, to be saved. I now ask you, Father, in Jesus Name, to open our eyes of understanding, so we can see what Jesus has done for us. Open our ears to hear the Holy Spirit speak to us, and renew in us a right spirit, so we can make a decision for the Lord. Break the assignment the enemy has over our life. Deliver us from the lies of the enemy, for it is written, we shall know the truth and the Truth will set us free. Amen

If you or anyone who ask Jesus into your heart, he will move heaven and earth to come. You have to want him more than you want life itself. Father is for you, now against you. He wants you to have abundant life. Anything less is not his will.

Supernatural or Supra-natural?

I had a supra-natural encounter with the angel of the Lord. I was not a believer, did not go to church, and did not have any friends who went to church. I did not allow anyone who was a believer to witness to me. I had a word for them, "How do you know for sure what you believe is correct?" If they couldn't answer me quickly, I would tell them, 'there is the door, don't come back.' I remember one lady who came to the house one evening. She sat down with her books, bible, and asked me, "Are you saved?" I asked, "Saved from what?" Her eyes got really big as she opened her book, and bible side by side. She tried again, "Are you going to heaven?" I said, "Not anytime soon. I am only twenty. I have no plans for heaven." She took a deep breath and ran her finger down the page of her book. She said, "All have sinned…" I started laughing and said, "You got that right. The world is flat out sinning every day and nothing is stopping it." I stopped laughing when I saw the tears in her eyes. My dad walked into the room and said, "What's going on here?" She said, "Do you know the Lord?" He looked at her for a moment, shook his head, as he said, "Don't think I met any Lords in this neighborhood. Does he live around here? Joy, do you know him?" I said, "No, and I don't think she does either." She closed her book and bible and apologized for coming to our house. Dad told her not to apologize, she had not done anything to apologize for. I felt sorry for her and wondered why she wasn't able to stand up for what she believed, if she really believed it. This was how far from the Lord I was, when the supra-natural encounter took place.

In 1972, the angel of the Lord met me face to face in a drycleaners. He preceded to tell me about what people all over the world were doing to save themselves, working to get saved, working to stay saved, doing legalistic things to confirm they were saved, keeping the traditions of their elders. He told me religion would kill you, only a relationship with the Lord Jesus Christ would get you saved, and keep you saved. Salvation was a free gift. He asked me to read a book by Hal Lindsey, because 'Hal knew God', and if I would read Hal's book, Satan is Alive and Living on Planet Earth, I would never see him here again. He didn't tell me I would get saved, only I would never see him again here. So I read the book, and the night I read it, I got saved and filled with the Spirit of the Lord. Within an hour after the Lord saved me, he sent a lady, I had never met, to invite me to her church. She didn't live in the same town as I did. She drove a long way that night, to wash her clothes in the laundry matt where I was working, to invite me to go to church with her, after I got saved. She said, "My father is the Senior Pastor of the church right behind this place of business. The Lord sent me to invite you to meet me there Sunday morning." I agreed to meet her, and went to church there till we moved to another city several years later. God is a supra-natural God. I did not say a supernatural God. For God is not supernatural at all. The word supernatural means – of or pertaining to the existence outside the natural world. Especially, not attributable to natural forces. Attributed to the exercise of divine power, miraculous. God is more than that. Demons do supernatural things, like when Moses threw his rod down, Moses performed a supernatural event. The priest of Pharaoh did the same thing, and Moses rod which became a serpent, ate up the serpent-rods of pharaoh. So if the priest can do what Moses did, how were they doing it? Moses did a supra-natural act. His rod serpent, ate up the supernatural act of the priest. A supernatural act of demons? If demons, and man can perform supernatural acts, God has to be above the act of demons and devils. I looked up the word **Supra** and **it means above and over, greater than, preceding.**

God is supra-natural, which means; He is above and over, greater than demons, devils and mankind. He is the Eternal God, who created the supernatural. Man and demons can perform the supernatural, but only God can work outside the supernatural, that is why He is God.

Jesus said, "I am the true vine and my Father is the husbandman. What is a husbandman? 1092 in Hebrew/Greek- It is a farmer. What do farmers do? They plow the field, they sow the seed, and they harvest the crop. We need to read the Word closely, and listen to the Holy Spirit speaking to us. When someone tells us: look what Jesus is doing in a certain situation, we better pay attention to give God all the glory. It is not us doing the act, when it is impossible for a human to do it. A friend related a story to me, about a church collecting several thousand dollars, and making it possible for a ministry to get a well dug in another country. They also made up enough money out of a small number of people to get a solar powered pump put in to pump the water. She said, "The Lord told me, *'we had given Him a drink of water,'* when we provided the money to pay for a pump, so these people could have water in their church and school." When it was related to the church it came out, "We provided water to the ministry by providing the money to the ministry." She said, the entire church missed the blessing, because the church took the credit for providing the money instead of giving God the glory. People fail to hear the Spirit speaking when the Lord says, '*You provided me a drink of water,*' by providing these folks with a well and power to pump it."

When we take the glory, the credit for what God is doing, we are walking in the flesh and not the Spirit. Sad to say, a lot of people, including preachers are walking in the flesh, and don't even realize it, by taking the credit for what God is doing among His people. Our job is to listen to the Spirit, so we can relay what the Spirit is saying, instead of saying what we think about a situation.

Purity is a choice.

In Matthew 5:8, God gave us a powerful word about Him. This scripture tells us, if we want to see God, we have to be pure in heart. 'Blessed are the pure in heart, for they shall see God.' Pure is important to God, so it should be important to us. The dictionary states the word pure means, free from impurities', defilements, or pollutions, not mixed, clean. The Greek meaning is clean, clear, and pure. The thing with pure is, you can't make yourself that way, because you were born in sin. Only a supra-natural God can do it for you. Only He can purify you to the state, where you can see Him, hear Him and obey Him. So how do you get the purity necessary to see God? You have to want to want the truth more than you want the things of this world. He will come to you, and He will purify you, so you can know and see Him.

Many several years ago, I witnessed an example of seeing God. I had a mercury that I drove. No one except me drove that car. My husband didn't like the vehicle, he had a truck he drove, so we just didn't share driving each other's vehicle. I didn't allow anyone to drive my car, because it was my prayer closet. I would sit in my car praying, reading my bible and worship. My husband never drove it, because he said the car was haunted by a ghost. It felt strange to him, when he got in the car with me. One Sunday morning, when I was leaving for church, I cranked the car, sat for a few minutes praying, before I left the driveway. I backed out, at the end of the driveway, when I put on the brakes to stop, the pedal went to the floorboard of the car, before it stopped. When I got to the stop sign, the brake pedal went to the floor, before it stopped. It happened again at the two red lights, before the turn to go to the church building. I asked the Lord, "is that normal?" but I was at church, and hurried to get into the building. I forgot all about it when I got inside, to my Sunday school class. As I was leaving, someone stopped me to talk. I remembered the pedal and asked the individual about it. She stated, "I don't know, I have never paid attention to how far that peddle goes down, when I put on the brakes." Before I drove home, I prayed asking God to give His angels charge over me and the car. I was not sure if something was wrong or if that was normal. I was trusting God to get me home safely. When I went in, fixed lunch, I casually mentioned the brake pedal going to the floorboard of the car. before it stopped. My husband looked at me like I was crazy and said, "That is not normal. I don't think there is anything wrong with that car, but I will take it to the brake repair shop in the morning to have it checked out. You can't go to church tonight." He was leaving for work at three in the afternoon, and I would not have a vehicle to get to church. I prayed about it after he left. I sat, read my bible for an hour, before church started. I felt like, since 'there was nothing wrong with the car,' I could drive it to church, and he could take it tomorrow morning to have it checked out.

I got my bible, and got in the car. I prayed, "Lord, this is your vehicle. We have spent a lot of time together in it, I know I am safe in you, and in this vehicle. I turn this car over to your protective care, in Jesus name." I drove to church. It did the same thing at every stop sign, and red light, and when I pulled up to park, at the church. It did the same thing going home. The vehicle stopped, when the pedal hit the floorboard. Church was wonderful, Father had met us and we worshiped Him.

That night I slept peacefully and dreamless. When I woke up the next morning, the car and my husband were gone. He had taken the car before I woke up, and gone to have it looked at. Four hours later, he came home. He was very quiet, hardly spoke a word to me, as he went to the bathroom, came back, and sat down in the chair across from me. I looked up at him, and he said, "How long has the car been stopping for you?" I laughed and said, "Since I bought it." He shook his head, tried again, "I mean, how long the pedal has been hitting the floor before it stopped?" I didn't know, I had not noticed it until yesterday morning and told him so. He said, "You are crazy. The brake lines were bone dry. When they put it up on the rack, opened the drums, and checked the lines, there was a hole in the major brake line. There was no brake fluid in the lines or the drums. I had to use the emergency brakes, and drive ten miles an hour to get the car to the repair shop. The manager wanted to know why I didn't have it towed in. Driving it was impossible. I told him it was my wife's car, and I just found out yesterday, about the brakes not holding." He said, "Your wife is lucky to be alive. How long has it been since she drove it?" When I told him you drove it to church yesterday morning, he said 'that was impossible, because the car would never have stopped, there was no fluid in the lines.' I grinned and said, "Well, Jesus was with me, because I drove it to church last night, and it stopped every time for me." The anger in his eyes was there to see, his voice got soft, as he said, "And I don't believe you. You could have been killed driving that car. It almost killed me driving it to the shop. I could not stop it. I hit the bank across the street, and if a car had been coming at the stop sign, it would have hit me. I could not stop the car, and ran straight through the sign. I had to use the emergency brake to stop it, and drive ten miles an hour to get that car a mile and a half up the road. Here you are, telling me you drove it yesterday, twice to church, over four miles away, and it stopped every time?" "Yes. Jesus is with me. He protects and watches over me. I am His child, and that is His job." He got up, shaking his head, and didn't speak to me the rest of the day. He left for work still not talking to me. I prayed for him, and I thanked God for His loving protection. I thanked Him for the ability to see Him working in my life.

That was a supra-natural act of God. A car with no brake fluid should not stop, but my car did, because God is more than able to do that which we think not.

Another example of God at work in my life that affected several people.

My husband, his brother, his wife and I took a trip to Colorado. We drove across country together, taking turns driving. That evening, we were somewhere in Kansas, we pulled off the interstate to have a bite to eat, use the restroom and stretch our legs. When we pulled off, we saw a huge oak tree next to a service station. Martha and I commented, how huge it was, and how full and pretty it was. We went in, washed our hand, used the restroom, and got us all cold drinks. We had packed a lunch for our first meal to save money. She and I were 'pray- ers' and we prayed over our meal, asking Father to keep us safe on the entire trip. We thanked him for our food, this beautiful spot to eat our packed lunch, and all the beautiful sights we were seeing along the way. We all laughed, talked and had a great time together. When we finished our meal, she and I went back to the bathroom to relieve ourselves of the drinks, and wash our hands. We got to talking about what a wonderful trip this was going to be, and how happy our husbands were about getting to go to Colorado. We changed drivers, as we started out, so my husband and I could sleep. It was getting dark and we had driven the first lap all day. They were going to do the night and morning, till six a.m. After breakfast, we would change drivers, and we would drive, so they could sleep. Sometime near five a.m., I felt her take hold of my hand. I opened my eyes and saw tears running down her cheeks. She squeezed my hand with her left hand, I looked at her hand, and her wedding rings were missing. I knew what had happened. She had left them in the bathroom of the station yesterday evening, when we had gone back to wash our hands.

She and I can talk without saying words. I shook my head, and silently began to pray in the Spirit. At five-thirty a.m., she said to all of us, "Wake up and let's find someplace to eat breakfast." My husband woke up, and said, "I want the biggest cup of black coffee you can find, don't worry about food." Everyone laughed, as we watched for an exit that had any place to eat breakfast.

We pulled into a truck stop. Her husband said, "Truck stops have the best food. We will try this place, I bet they got good coffee!" She and I went to the restroom to wash our hands. She had tears in her eyes, as she washed her hands, telling me what I already knew. "I left them on the back of the sink at that service station restroom. I took them off, when I washed my hand, lay them on the back of the sink, and I just forgot them. I will tell him at breakfast, he will probably be mad. He just purchased them for me for our anniversary last year." I told her when I was praying, the Lord had spoken to me and told me, "If you both will ask, I will restore the rings. Give me glory for restoration." She said, "What does that mean?" I said, "It means, when you tell our husbands at breakfast, you accidentally left them in the station restroom that you believe God will restore them, He will, if we all pray and agree. God will restore them too you. They will be there when we come back through in five days. Five is the number of grace, and God's grace is sufficient for you in this matter. Give God all the glory for what He is going to do for you in restoring the rings." She smiled and agreed. Then she said, "Do you remember what exit we were at when we stopped?" I said, "No, but God does."

At breakfast she broke the news, and it didn't go too well to start with. Neither of our husbands could believe God would restore the rings. Neither of them knew what exit it was, we turned off to get gas, and neither of them thought anyone would turn those expensive rings into an attendant, or that the attendant would keep them for someone to come back after them. 'That was impossible,' they both agreed.

I told them what I heard the Holy Spirit speak to me, as I prayed. They just stared at me, sat quietly, as I talked. They both looked at her and said, "What do you think?" She smiled and agreed with me, God would restore the rings, if we all agreed, He would do it. They looked at each other and said, "Ok, we agree with you both. We will see it happen when we come back through, if we can find the station we pulled off at." We all shook hands together, finished our breakfast. They got large cups of coffee to go, and we started out to our destination on the opposite side of the Rocky Mountains. We spent four days seeing the sights, visiting their brother and his wife, going to the Mesa to look out over the wonderful world below. On the fourth evening, we packed our bags, and left early evening. My husband and I were driving the first night and early morning. They were driving the day, so they could watch for a sign, they might recognize, to let them know it was the right exit. I was so tired from the night driving, I could barely wait to get in the back seat, and fall asleep. My husband lay his pillow against the corner window, and was asleep in minutes. I lay my head on my pillow in his lap, and was asleep immediately.

I dreamed this dream. I saw a huge oak tree with glistening lights in the top of the tree. The sun was shining brightly, and a fog was lifting from the ground making everything look ghostly and strange. When I woke up at lunch time, I told her what I dreamed. I stayed awake after lunch.

We ran into a storm with lightning, thunder, and lots of fog, off and on. When the rain stopped, and fog lifted, we were amazed at how beautiful everything was. She saw a double rainbow in a field to the left of the road, and called everyone's attention to it. I said, "Look at how the rainbow keeps going over the tops of the trees, and how sparkling everything looks, just like my dream." We ran into another fog, and had to slow down to a crawl, to be able to see the road. As we came out of the fog, we saw the rainbow looked like it came down in the top of a big oak tree. She started hollering, "Take the next exit, take the next exit. I believe we are at the right exit." Her husband took the next exit, turned left over the expressway, and followed the rainbow. On the right, just past the big oak tree was the station we stopped at. We all started laughing and rejoicing. Her husband said, "Don't get your hopes up just yet. I will go in and ask." I said, "God has restored the rings, and they are here waiting." She said, "I believe I will get them back." My husband said, "I sure hope so." Her husband went into the station. When he came out, he was looking at the ground sadly. He walked up to her, looked up and smiled, reached out, handed her the wedding rings. I jumped, I shouted, I hugged everyone, I praised God loudly with my voice. My husband grabbed me, hugged me, telling me to hush being so loud. I could not help it. She began to cry, as she put her rings on, as she said, "I give you glory, and thank you Lord, for restoring my wedding rings to me."

The attendant told her husband, a woman had found the rings that evening, and had brought them to him, because she felt the rings were expensive, and someone would be looking for them. She knew how she would feel, if it happened to her. We knew she was a Christian woman. The attendant told her, he would keep the rings for seven days, if no one came back to get them, she could come back and get them. We knew he was a Christian man, he knew someone would be looking for them. Tomorrow was the day, the other lady was supposed to come back, and get the rings. He knew she would be happy the real owner had gotten her rings back.

This was a supra-natural act of God.

What is the key to having a supra-natural act of God take place in your life? The key is hearing the Holy Spirit speaking to you in your Spirit. A lot of times, He is speaking, we aren't listening. We are too busy with the cares of this world, or we are so double-minded about what we believe, we fail to heed the still small voice of God. Did seeing this change our husbands? No, they were not seeing or hearing in the spirit realm, and they soon forgot what they beheld. How many little things take place, do we miss, because we fail to listen in the spirit realm, we fail to see in the spirit realm?

Well, I hear someone saying? Can you give another personal situation, you were personally involved in that is a supra-natural move of the living God?

In the 1990's, my husband had a heart attack. He was on the way to work one morning. He stopped at the local convenient store to get a cup of coffee. He told me, he came out of the store holding the coffee, half way to the car, and he felt a sharp pain in his back. He walked quickly to the car, opened the door, sat down with his legs outside the car. He had dropped the coffee on the ground. As he bent over, when suddenly, another sharp pain hit him in the chest. He was opening a little bottle of nitroglycerin, to put under his tongue, when another pain hit him in the back. He dropped the bottle, but bent over, picked up three pills off the ground, and put them under his tongue. He told us the next thing he remembered, was waking up in the emergency room, with doctors all over him. How did he get to the hospital? He does not know, but an EMT who got him out of the car said, "He drove himself to the hospital." I told the EMT, 'we live in Powder Springs, Georgia, that is impossible for an unconscious man to drive himself to the Piedmont hospital in Atlanta.' The EMT said, "I was getting my ambulance ready to leave, when his car pulled up in the parking lot at the emergency room door. The horn started blowing. I walked over to the car, because I could not see anybody in the car. When I got to the door, he was laying over. The engine was still running, the horn was blowing, and he was out cold. I turned the engine off, as I pulled him from the car, and lay him on the ground. Someone came running with a stretcher, and we lifted him on to the unit, and took him into the emergency room. He didn't come too, until we put him on oxygen, and gave him a shot to revive him. I moved his car to a parking place, and came back to see if I could get a number to call someone to come to the hospital in case, he didn't make it. They found your number in his billfold." My husband said, he didn't remember driving the car to the hospital. He didn't remember anything from the time he tried to pick up the medicine off the ground. He told me, he asked God to help him, and that is the last he remembers. From where he had the heart attack to the hospital is between twenty-two to twenty-five miles, with lots of red lights, turns, and traffic. The doctor who took care of him told us, he could not have driven anything, anywhere, after the initial attack hit him. My God is able. He gives his angels charge over me and my family. I told my husband his angel drove him to the emergency room, and had someone waiting in the area at the door to get him out of his car. His life was in the hands of the Lord, and the Lord had a supra-natural event planned for him that day.

I want to stop here, and thank the Lord for what He has done, is doing, and shall do in our life. Thank you, Lord! I give you all the glory for who You are. I give You thanks for who I am, in You.

Another event concerning my husband: He had his first heart attack in 1985. He was at work, felt sick and left coming home. He never made it. On the way, he passed a hospital, and thought he should stop, and see how bad this really was. When he parked his truck, and got out, a sharp pain hit his left arm and chest. He passed out in the parking lot between his truck and another truck. He said, 'he didn't know how long he lay there before he came too, but it was daylight when he passed out.' It was dark when he came too, got up and made his way into the hospital emergency room, falling over the desk saying, "I'm having a heart attack." The nurse grabbed him by the shirt to keep him from falling backwards, held him till another nurse got a wheel chair behind him. He had three heart attacks, and went into a coma. When the doctor called me at home at 11:00 pm, he asked me to come immediately, it was critical. My husband had not woke up in the two hours since he was admitted. He asked me to call in his family. I called his brother and let him know he was in a coma at the hospital above our house. I was on my way, a neighbor was driving me, and she would keep our daughter.

When I arrived at the hospital, the doctor met me in a little room. He wanted to let me know there was no change in his condition. They were unable to get his boots off, because his feet were stiff, and they didn't want to cause any damage by forcing them off his feet. He had told a nurse when he was lucid, he wanted to die with his boots on. I asked if I could go back to ICU to see him. The doctor said, "No. He isn't awake and there is nothing you can do." I said, "I can pray. I can lay my hands on him and pray." He said, "No. not right now." The Spirit in me flared, and I said, "Oh, yes, NOW! He needs me now, and I will go back, lay hands on him and pray for him." He asked the nurse to get me a shot, because I was out of control. I told the doctor, 'I wasn't out of control, I wanted to see my husband, and I would see him now.' He walked away, telling the nurse to handle me. She took me in her arms and said, "Now honey, I know how stressful this is too you, but he is critical, and you can't go back." I stood still and asked her, "If he were your husband, what would you do?" She smiled, took my hand saying, "Follow me." She took me back to the ICU room, took me in, and stood at the curtained-door watching. I walked over to him, kissed him on the forehead, laid my hand on his chest and firmly said, "You will live and not die by the authority of the Lord Jesus Christ. Wake up, in Jesus Name!" He opened his eyes, and smiled at me saying, "Hey, I don't feel too good." I smiled, looked at the nurse, told her we would get his boots and clothes off now. She should get a gown to put on him, and he would be ready for whatever they needed to do next. She said, "I have his gown under the bed he is laying on. I left it there, just in case." He let me undress him with her help, and put the gown on him. She called the doctor, and told him, "Your patient is awake. You need to come take care of him." I told her I would leave, so she wouldn't get into trouble. She smiled, as she said, "I don't care if I do. What I just witnessed is worth all the trouble I could get into." I went to the waiting room to wait for my brother-n-law and his wife. They arrived after about thirty minutes. I told them what happened. Martha smiled and said, "We need to keep praying." The hospital transported him to another hospital in the city for a heart cauterization the following day. They had to put two stints in his heart. For the next ten years, he had a heart attack every year; the week before Thanksgiving or Christmas, spending the holidays in the hospital.

In May 2011, he was put in the hospital for a laser cauterization for a closure of the main back artery. His doctor told him when that artery closed, or reached 90%, he would die. He was at 93%, so they used him for a test to see if they could do it, and have a patient live. At the time, he was the only living patient to go through the surgery, and live with no side effects at all. A close friend had the same surgery, and did not make it. God's plans are higher than ours, His thought are not our thoughts, and He does what pleases Him in all the earth. For thou O Lord, has made me glad through your works: I will triumph in the works of your hands. O, Lord, how great are your works! And your thoughts are very deep.

The Lord has a plan, we don't know the plan, but God does. I don't know why God has not healed him. We have prayed for complete healing, but it has not come. More than one doctor has told us, "You are a walking miracle. You should have died years ago, but here you are a walking miracle." In August 2014, his pulmonary cardiologist told him, "You are a true miracle walking. All your arteries are in major closure, heart, legs, neck and you are walking around while others in your condition are in the hospital dying."

I often wonder why it is so hard for people to believe. I go back to the days when I didn't believe. I try to remember why it took me so many years to allow the Lord to work in my life, and show me who He really was. I can remember the many times different people tried to talk to me about the Lord, and I would avoid the discussion. I would be rude, and short with them. When I lost the two babies, within two years of each other, and realized I would never have a child, I still didn't want to listen. I would not go around people who were Christian's, or take any kind of time to watch TV preachers. My granny, who lived in Alabama, told me more than once, she was praying for me. I now believe she is the reason I got radically saved, that night at the drycleaners.

The night, I got saved was a supra-natural event. Two weeks before that night, I had an encounter with the Angel of the Lord.

I had put in several applications, and had no responses to any of them. I was tired of looking for a job. I went driving through the small town near my house in the opposite direction from all my last trips, putting in applications. As I drove through the backstreet, I saw a sign in the window of a small dry cleaner. It had a washer dryer area attached to the side of the cleaners. I pulled in and asked the attendant if they were hiring. She said, "Yes, we are, I am looking for a night clerk to work from three to eleven, five days a week. No weekends, I have a weekend person. Are you interested?"

I told her I was interested, as I asked her what the pay was. She said, "Five dollars an hour, eight hours a day. If you take twenty minutes for lunch break, you get paid for it, if you don't take a whole half hour." I told her I would take it, didn't need any more information. When did she want me to come to work? She said, "how about tomorrow?" I told her I would be there with bells on. She laughed, handed me an application, telling me to fill it out. I went to work the next afternoon at three p.m.

I met the owner of the drycleaners. He was a really nice guy, same age as me. He was married with a four year old daughter. He wanted to know, if I would like to make some extra money baby-sitting his daughter, from eleven am to three pm each day. It would be temporary till his wife could find a nursery to put her in. I accepted the job, and made twenty extra dollars a day for three months. His little darling had an imaginary friend that had to have a plate of food set at the table during lunch, with a half glass of milk. As soon as, she left the table, I ate the friend's lunch. When she came back, she would clap her hands, and tell me how much she loved her friend. She was so busy talking to me, she never realized it was me, who ate the food for three months. I was happy taking care of Jack's little girl.

Paige, was a cute and sweet child. She was easy to tend to, and enjoyed stories, games, walking around the house looking for her imaginary friend. She would sit, and listen to me read storybooks too her, and then try to retell me the story. I enjoyed her while I kept her. I missed her when she went to nursery school, I was sad to see her go to nursery school. I would have kept her for free, she was so much fun to be around.

My heart still yearned for a baby.

I loved my job, and the people I worked for. I wasn't lonely anymore. I was happy for a change. I got caught up in my job, the people I was meeting who came in regularly to wash clothes, and/or bring in their dry cleaning. I had lots of people to talk too on a regular basis. I had been working about a year, when Eve decided she was going to change a few things. She wanted to clean the washer/dryer area before she left in the afternoon, so I had nothing to do, but take care of drycleaner side. Customers were more important than cleaning washing machines, floors and filling up coke machines. That was fine with me, so she took over that chore. She also wanted to swap the sewing chores, and gave those to me instead of her having to do them all during the day. I accepted that. I loved to sew.

I arrived at work one Friday evening at three pm, and was ready to walk out the door, as I arrived. She was holding the keys to the front door, and handed them to me as I walked in. She said, 'she had a lot of running around to do before dark, there was a radio in the back, I could turn on to keep me company, if I got lonely.' I told her I would rather read than listen to the radio. She said, "I left it on in case you needed something to listen too, besides the silence in this place, you can turn it off, before you leave tonight."

Around four-fifteen, the sky began to cloud up. I heard a big clap of thunder, but saw no lightening. I thought that was strange, the sky should have lit up, because in my mind, lightening causes the sound of thunder. The thunder sound was so loud, it shook the windows. Within fifteen minutes, it was raining cats and dogs. The lightening showed up with a vengeance, running across the sky without stop, with non-stop thundering sounds. The wind was blowing sideways, instead of coming down straight. I wondered if we were having a tornado. I went to the back of the building, to try to turn the radio back on, all I got was static. When I got back to the front of the building, I saw the laundry-mat door blowing wide open, and rain pelting the cement floor. I ran to get the key to lock the door, so the rain could not blow in. I got the mop and bucket, to mop the floor dry. The door to the drycleaners was blowing open, and the buzzer was ringing non-stop. The door could be pulled out for anyone who wanted to come in, so I pushed a big trashcan against it, to keep it from blowing inward. The buzzer would ring either way, so as to alert me someone was coming in. I mopped the floor, and turned on the fan to dry it quickly.

This storm was getting on my last nerve. The phone rang suddenly, but when I answered it, no one was there. I decided to finish cleaning the floors on the dry cleaner side, and get all the dirty clothes pinned for dry cleaning or washing. No one was going to come in with this storm raging. I finished all the clothes, took them to the buggy, and pushed them to the back. I decided to sit down, and read a book. I checked both sides to make sure all doors were locked, and that no one was in the bathrooms, before I sat down. I did not want someone sneaking up on me. I sat down in the rickety chair behind the counter, and rummaged under the counter for something to read. Junk and magazines, I had read before fell to the floor. I wanted to kick the stuff under the counter, but decided it would be harder to clean up later than to pick it up now. I put it back where it fell from. Booming thunder and white streaking fire made me sit back, and stare out the windows into the night sky. I had never seen a storm quiet like this one. I really wanted to close up and go home. Nobody in their right mind would be out in this weather.

A magazine slipped from the stuffing, falling to the floor. I reached down picked it up. When I sat back up, there across the counter was a tall, tan man in a white lambskin jacket with the prettiest eyes, and smile I had ever seen. His eyes looked like the morning sky when the sun comes up, translucent blue with the whitest clouds. I almost fell out of my chair. His smile increased, as he took off his jacket. He had on a red shirt, dark jeans, with white tennis shoes, that were as clean as a pin. He wasn't wet at all. Strange, I thought, it is raining buckets and his coat isn't even damp. And the doorbell didn't ring. Every thought I was thinking disappeared in that smile.

"Yes, can I help you?" I heard myself saying. His smile got bigger, and I noticed how perfect his white teeth looked, almost like a pearl necklace strung together. "It is cold outside and raining. My coat pocket has come off. My hands are cold. I don't have any gloves. Do you do sewing here?"

"Well, yes, but it cost three dollars." I said quietly.

"I don't have any money," he said with that pearly white smile shining across his face. "Could you sew the pocket on for me?" I could sew anything on anything, but it still cost three dollars. I didn't own this establishment. There was no one around to ask, if it was ok to sew it for free. He smiled that consuming smile again, as he said, "It won't take long, and then I could be on my way." That was a good idea, him gone!

"Well," I said, "let me get a needle and thread. I will be right back. You can stand there. I will sit here and sew your pocket back on for you." I did, he did, and I knew it would not take, but a minute to get the pocket sewn back in place, and him out of here.

WRONG!

The coat was white lambskin. The pocket had holes that had to be matched to the holes in the coat, for the needle to go through the leather to reattach the pocket. He smiled, as he leaned against the huge glass window, and began to talk. I was somewhat scared, and yet I wasn't. I was alone in the business with no way out. I had personally locked all the doors, except the one right beside him, and he didn't act like he was going to move away from it, until he got his coat back.

As I sewed, he talked. He told me he had been all over the world, in every kind of church, synagogue, mosque, hut and building where people were talking about every kind of religion. He had found people were strange in the way they looked at God. This conversation was going to be one sided. I had to pay attention to what I was doing, or I would never get this pocket sewn back on this coat. "You have never been out of this country. You don't want to talk about God. You don't know

God." These were not questions. These were statements, as if he knew exactly what he was saying, and every word was true. No, I did not want to discuss God. I did not believe in God.

He preceded to tell me about the places he had been, the religions he had observed, and how religion will kill you. "There is no life in religion, it is a killer of people, and most people are in the kill. The whole world out there is looking for something to ease the pain. Even though some people beat themselves to appease their gods, thinking the pain they inflict upon themselves, would ease the pain within. The problem, he explained, is they are looking in the wrong place for God. God came to this earth to show Himself to the human race. They denied Him, because He didn't do what they expected Him to do for them. Set up a kingdom, and do away with the Romans. "Did you know some people kill animals and sacrifice to a god that will do absolutely nothing for them? Some people worship rocks, some trees, some snakes, some even worship cows, but it is all in vain….." he asked quietly.

The thunder and lightning was still raging, and getting louder by the second, but while he was talking, I did not notice it…..only when he was quiet…..I really didn't want to hear any more of this one sided conversation. What any of this had to do with me sewing his pocket on this jacket, I could not see. But I let him talk with an occasional grunt of attention. "Some people call themselves atheist. They fight against a god, they say, they don't believe in. Some folks go to church and sit, then leave exactly like they came, depressed, angry, cursing, drinking, filled with hatred one for another. They don't have ears to hear from God, so they never change."

Suddenly I had his pocket sewn back on. I was tying the thread in a double knot to make sure it stayed on his coat. "It is finished," I announced to him, as I slung the coat onto the counter top. As he picked the coat up, a pencil rolled off the counter….." That is a very nice job, thank you very much." I reached down to pick up the pencil off the floor, as I said, "You are welcome." When I stood back up, HE WAS GONE! He was not there standing in front of the window. The trashcan was still against the door, the bell had not made a sound. Where did he go? I looked frantically out the floor to ceiling windows, and he was nowhere on the street…and I could see in every direction, because of the street lights.

I was truly scared now. Scared to be alone, and I didn't care if I got fired, I was leaving right now, an hour before quitting time. I ran, turned off all the lights except the counter lights. I grabbed my coat, keys, pocket book and locked the doors, as quickly as I could. I left everything else, as it was. I didn't want to think about him ever again. When I got home, I ripped off my clothes, and climbed into bed. I immediately fell into a deep sleep. The next morning when I woke up, I did not give yesterday one thought. In fact, I didn't think about him again, until two weeks later.

To make a long story shorter, two weeks later, he came back on a night just like the previous time. The same things happened over again with the storm, he was not wet, the appearance out of nowhere, coat pocket off his jacket, everything except he started talking right where he left off the previous time. As he said, "Yes, some people worship rock, some trees, some even worship the dead. In India, they worship cows, in Russia, they don't want to believe in God, in Africa, some tribes worship the sky, moon, sun. You would not believe what some people worship. Some people are just religious and don't worship anything. They are dead as door knobs. It is tradition, ritual, what's expected, and they do exactly what is expected of them by their leaders. You don't believe in God, do you? You don't like to talk about it either, do you? But you do like to read books. What is your favorite book?" he asked quietly.

"Gone with the Wind." I answered.

"What kind of books do you like best?" he asked quietly.

"Novels." I said. Why is this taking me so long to sew this stupid pocket back on this dumb coat? I did it already! I know what to do, but I can't find the stupid little holes. I don't want to hear this!!!! I wanted to yell at him to go away, but I didn't. I wanted to see him disappear like magic, like he had appeared. I wanted to know what he was doing here, asking me stupid questions. I was afraid to ask, I was afraid, but I wasn't.

Then he changed the subject. "Do you know where a Christian bookstore is?"

"Yes," I replied, "there is one about a fourth of a mile from my house. In fact, it is close enough to walk to, but I have never been there. Why?"

"I want you to read a book and if you will read it, you will never see me again here."

"What is the name of the book?" I asked. I would read anything to keep him from coming back here.

"It is a very good book. You can find it at any Christian bookstore. I know you will love it. The name of it is; *Satan is Alive and, Living on Planet Earth.* It was written by Hal Lindsey, he knows God. If you will read it, I promise you will never see me here again."

"Ok, I will buy it and read it as soon as I can find it."

"Great! Remember, religion will kill you, but relationship with the Lord Jesus Christ, will give you eternal life!"

I double tied the knot again and said softly, in a whisper, "You better stay on this coat this time." I laid the jacket on the counter. A pencil rolled off the counter. I reached down to pick it up, and knew before I stood up, he would not be there, yet it still scared me. I grabbed my coat, pocketbook, key to lock the doors. I hurriedly turned off all the lights, and left an hour before I was to get off from work. It was still raining, lightning, thundering, but I had not heard any of it while he was talking to me. All I heard was, "If you read it, you will never see me here again."

The next morning I woke up early, put on my clothes, got on my coat, tennis shoes and a ten dollar bill. I walked to the Christian bookstore. It was a beautiful morning, clear, cool with the sun shiny bright. I needed the exercise. I placed my keys in my left pocket, and the ten dollar bill in the right pocket. It did not seem like a long walk. I felt like a weight was being lifted off my shoulders. The lady behind the counter was waiting on another customer when I went in, so I browsed the shelves looking for the Satan book. I am a fast reader, and I am a fast looker. I searched for half an hour, without finding anything by Hal Lindsey, whoever that man is.

I heard a door ringer go off. When I looked up, I saw the lady behind the counter was standing almost in front of me. "Can I help you find something?" she asked smiling. She had the sweetest voice I had ever heard. I smiled back and said, "Yes, I am looking for a book about Satan and it was written by Hal Lindsey." She laughed as she said, "Oh yes, we have that book. It is called, *Satan is Alive and Living on Planet Earth*. Come with me. We walked to an isle at the side of the store that had a sign printed with a word, I had never heard before: PROPHECY.

She looked and looked for the book, but when she was unable to find it, she said, "I will go to the back to see, if we have any more in stock. That book is a best seller, please excuse me." While she was gone, I continued to look through a table of books. I found one written by Pat Boone. I knew he was a singer on TV. I read the first chapter, while she was gone, and decided I would get this one, too.

She came back, telling me she didn't have any more of that book, but would order it for me. We went to the cash register, where she was going to ring up the purchase, and special order the book by Mr. Lindsey. Standing in front of her, I looked up at the top shelf behind her. I told her the book was on the top shelf behind her. She smiled, as she said, "We don't put books on the top of the cabinet, because I can't reach them." I pointed and she turned around looking at the top shelf. There on the top shelf was the book standing up, slightly open with the front of the book facing toward me. She went to get a ladder, climbed up, and retrieved the book for me.

"You are a special person. That book is not supposed to be there. It is the last book we have in stock. You are going to enjoy reading this one!" I handed her the ten dollar bill, as she was ringing it up. "That will be ten dollars and forty-five cents," she stated as she took the bill. "Oh, that is all the money I brought with me. I will have to put one book back." I said sadly. "No, no. Let me redo that. We are having a ten percent discount to all new customers this week. You did say this was the first time you have shopped with us, didn't you?" I didn't remember saying that, but it was my first time shopping in any Christian bookstore ever, so I nodded affirmative. I got back change, and left smiling like I had won a poker game. When I got home, I sat both books on the table, cooked my husband a bite to eat, and woke my husband. He had worked till five am, so he needed his sleep. He got up, took his shower and came to the table. I placed his breakfast in front of him, handing him a cup of coffee. He asked me where I had gotten the two books sitting on the table. I told him I had walked to the book store while he was asleep to purchase them. We ate our respective meals, as we discussed me spending my money on frivolous stuff. 'Didn't I want to save, so we could eventually buy a bigger house, and another new car? Mine was getting old.' I left for work before he did. I took the Satan book to work with me. If it was slow tonight, I would read it. When I got to work, Eve was standing at the door waiting for me, so she could get a meeting. She gave me the spiel that it had been slow all day. She had cleaned everything, so I didn't have anything to do, except take care of the customer's, when they came in.

As soon as she left, I sat down with the book and began to read. I loved to read, but I had never read anything about Satan before. This should be very interesting.

Around five thirty in the afternoon, I looked up and realized no one had come through the doors on either side. I wondered if the town had shut down and everybody went home. I pondered what I had just read, as I got my supper out of the refrigerator in back. This was a really interesting book, not real easy to read, because it wasn't what I expected it to be about. Some things were over my head a ways, but all in all, I was going to read this book no matter what. I didn't want another surprise visit. As I walked back to the front, I got a coke, sat down to continue reading. When I sat back down, I thought how uncomfortable this chair is to sit in. I knew nothing about Satan, except the name sounded like he was not such a nice guy. We didn't have television growing up. We still didn't watch much TV, because I like to read. And we never discussed anything about Satan. He just never came up in any of the conversations. I didn't go to church, so I never heard anyone preach about him. This book was free of trash, and dirty words. It was a very interesting book.

The first chapter was asking questions, I asked myself every day of my life. What is happening? Why is it happening? Where is it happening? The subtitles caught my eye:

'Millions of spiritual creatures walk the earth unseen, both when we wake and when we sleep." I had never thought about spiritual creatures before. I guess Satan is a spiritual creature, if he is real. You can't see him, so that must mean he is a spirit of some sort. I kept reading. No one came into the laundry matt, the entire time I was reading. I got lost in the story. I found myself sitting with the lecture groups, watching the lady with the unusual plaid skirt. I listened to her conversation, and wondered if there was such a thing, as a true psychic with powers. I almost jumped out of my skin, when the man blurted out, 'this is not of God. And if you don't reject this power, it will kill you!'

I was hooked on this book, and for the next hour, I was there, sitting in the wings of the seats, where the conversations were batted back, and forth on God and Satan, covens and witches, good and evil. Time flew by, still no one came in, and neither did the phone ring. I was so absorbed in the book, I would not have noticed if someone came in, unless they yelled at me. Coming to the end of chapter 4, I ran up against a statement that stopped me in my reading tracks.

Satan may have won the battle in the garden, but he has not won the war. He has already been defeated, and he knows it! However, he is going to use every tactic in his bag of deceptions, to keep as many individuals from knowing from knowing it, especially those who are believers in Jesus. He already has the unbelievers in his grasp, by blinding them to the good news of the pardon, God freely offers through Jesus Christ. If the Good News we preach is hidden to anyone, it is hidden from the one who is on the road to eternal death. Satan, who is the god of this evil world, has made him blind, unable to see the glorious light of the gospel, that is shining upon him, or to understand the amazing message, we preach about the glory of Christ, who is God."

2 Corinthians 4:3-4, living bible.* Hal Lindsey

The following few sentences of his book changed my life:

"Where do you stand in this conflict? Perhaps you're having trouble accepting these things. If you are, guess who is helping you think that way? The most important thing to realize is, you don't have to believe everything to become a member of God's family. All you need is faith enough to call out to God in your heart, and thank Him, Jesus Christ died for your inability to measure up to His perfect standards. Receive the forgiveness of your sins, and thank Him for it. Tell Jesus Christ you want Him to come into your life right now, and begin to make it pleasing to God. If you did this, on the authority of God's Word. I assure you that you have eternal life right now."   Hall Lindsey – *Satan is Alive, and Living on Planet Earth*

I looked up the word assure. It refers to persons, and it alone has the sense of setting a person's mind at rest, with a view of removing doubt. To cause to feel sure, confident, to make certain, to give confidence. (American heritage Dictionary of the English Language)

I was not sure, nor did I have confidence this was true. I wondered how anyone could KNOW for sure or be without doubt. Right then, this was a ridiculous statement. Too ridiculous to be true, was it not? How can so many people be lost, if, it is this easy to be saved, I wondered out loud? I read the paragraph again, and thought how stupid we were, if this is true. Heaven could be that close, just by believing God loves you, and He allowed Jesus to die on the cross for you personally and individually. All you had to do was repent, ask the Father to forgive you, ask Jesus to come into your heart and make it pleasing to the Father.

Deception is a heinous thing. You can think you know the truth, and not have clue about the truth. You can think you are doing all the right things, are on your way to heaven, only to die and arrive in a burning hell. "How can anyone know you are not deceived?" I said out loud. What makes this paragraph true, and others not, how is it possible to be saved, and go to heaven, and *know for sure?* I NEEDED to know the answer to these questions. I WANTED to know the truth. There was a desire in me, calling out to know the Truth. I wanted to know it now.

I read, again, the paragraph, arguing with each statement, this was just too easy, so easy that everyone in the world could get saved, if they would only do what this says. I read it again, and still nothing happened. I didn't get the understanding, still could not believe, it was so easy. I said out loud, "I am going to read this aloud. I am going to say it, as a prayer, because I don't know how to pray. I have never done it before, and I want to know the truth. I opened my mouth saying, "Lord, I am calling out to you Father God. I thank you Jesus Christ died for my inabilities to measure up to your perfect standards. I know I am a sinner. I receive the forgiveness of my sins, and thank you for saving me. Jesus, I want you to come into my heart right now, and begin to make it pleasing to God. I believe. Amen.

Immediately, without warning, the book fell from my hands, I fell backwards against the wall, both feet went flying out in front of me. I was sitting in the chair, but I was stuck like glue to the wall. It felt like someone had removed a portion of the top of my head and was pouring hot oil through the top of my head. It was rushing down to the tips of my toes, up and out of my fingers; the sensation was like being washed up and down with hot oil and cold water. I was laughing, crying, and shaking like a leaf in a tornado. This seemed to go on for a very long time, yet when it stopped, only minutes had passed. I heard a voice speak to me, saying, "See my dear Child, I am Jesus, the Truth, the Way, the Life. You are mine and I am yours. I will never leave you nor forsake you. I will be with you all the days of your life."

"Yes, Lord!" came out of my mouth. I was so happy. I was filled with joy. I was light as a feather. I had never felt this good in my life. And the voice.....the Voice was so sweet, tender and it felt like it stayed inside me. I felt like I was new all over. Tears were still running down my cheeks. I could not stop smiling. I wanted to hug somebody, tell them what had happened to me, but there was no one around. So I started talking to the Lord out loud. I said, "Lord, I need to go to church to learn about you, you and who we are together. Lord, send someone to show me a church to go to." I had gone from unbeliever to believer in a matter of God's time. I had gone to work an unbeliever with no believing friends or immediate family, to believing that Jesus is alive and living in me, because He said so, when I prayed the prayer. I know, I know that I know HE IS GOD. Nobody had to convince me. Jesus convinced me, as He spoke to me. I *heard* His voice. That voice has never left me, since that December night, I got radically saved.

SPIRIT Filled

When someone starts talking about being Spirit filled, or filled with the Spirit, or baptism in the Spirit, people don't understand what you are talking about. The ones who do, are so varied in what they believe, it can turn into a free for all, when the words start flying.

When the Holy Spirit filled me with the power of God, the wisdom of God, the standard of God, the comfort of God, I didn't have any questions. I was not 'churched' and had no idea what it was. I read the bible, and He taught me, answered my questions that came up. The night I was born of the Spirit of God, He came to live inside of me. His Word was living inside of me. What I was reading, lined up with what I was hearing the Holy Spirit telling me. I have, over the years, heard many preachers preach, "Let's invite the Holy Spirit to come, stir us up, and fill us up." I wonder where their Holy Spirit lives every time, I hear someone say that. I don't have to invite the Holy Spirit to come stir me up. He lives inside of me twenty-four-seven. He never leaves, and He is always stirred up, all ways teaching me, all ways speaking, all ways filling me with wisdom, power, and the ability to do what He tells me to do. Sometimes, I have failed to allow Him to have first place by the choices I make. I admit that I have taken the initiative, and stepped over the boundary's He placed before me, and gone past the line to have my own way. It always turned out bad. But Father is faithful, even when I am not. He has never left me, nor forsaken me. He picked me up out of the pig-pen I jumped into, cleaned me up, and set me back on the right narrow path. He loves me, protects me, rescues me, cleanses me, speaks to me, corrects me, comforts me, reveals things to me that I am doing wrong. The sin nature is dying, because I want it to die. The sin nature is being taken over by a new nature that has full reign, because I know the Word washes me daily from all unrighteousness, and is taking down strongholds, I now hate, rather than hold on too.

Having an ear to hear the Spirit means, you listen when He speaks, you obey what He says, and do it. The scripture in John chapter 2 where Mary tells the disciples, "Whatever He says unto you, DO IT," is relevant to us today. Hearing with the ear of the Spirit is two parts. One, you have to be born again. I could not hear what the Spirit of the Lord was saying to me, until the night I repented of my sins. I could not hear, because my ear was attuned to the sound of what is going on in this world. The prince of the power of the air had tuned my ear, since the water birth from my mother. I could only hear what was taking place in the five senses. On the night of my born-again experience, when I encountered the Prince of Peace, He gave me a new ear, and spoke to me immediately, as His Spirit invaded all the souls' realm, and cleaned out the temple, so He could abide in me. Two, you have to obey what you hear the Spirit say to you. If you don't, you are not completing the cycle of birth. You have to be born-again to hear, but if you don't obey, you are still dead. Faith without works is dead, according to James. Do you know what a still-birth is? Look it up, you will be surprised at what you learn.

Most people do not have a clue what it means to have a Holy Spirit encounter. To begin with, many people do not believe the Holy Spirit is who He is. Who is He, you ask? I am glad you asked.

The Holy Spirit is the Spirit of God that moved upon the waters in the beginning, and everything that was created came into being by the Word of God. Gen. 1:2.

He is the Spirit of the Lord who will not all ways strive with man, Gen. 6:3.

He is the Spirit who lives in man, Gen 41:38, Ex 31:3, Num. 27:18, Isa 42:1.

He is the Spirit of the Lord who lifts up a standard against you, Isa. 59:19.

He got Mary pregnant. Jesus Christ is the child of the Holy Ghost, Mat. 1:18.

The Holy Spirit is, the HOLY Ghost is, the baptizer, Mat. 3:11.

The Holy Ghost speaks through man, Mark 13:11, Matt 10:20.

He is the teacher who teaches you what to say, Luke 12:12.

The Holy Spirit is Truth, John 15:26.

He is the comforter, John 14:16.

God reveals things by the Holy Ghost, 1 Corinthians 2:10.

The Holy Spirit forbids us to do things, Acts 16:6.

He is the power of Father God, Rom. 15:19

The Word of God gives witness to who the Holy Spirit is. He is God, just as Jesus is God. The Father is God.

No, not three God's, but One God manifest in three personages. *If you have seen Jesus, you have seen the Father, John 1:1*

John 14:9 – 14 - tells you if you have seen Jesus, you have seen the Father.

Religion

Any religion that says, God has no son, does not know the truth. They are deceived and are destined to hell. The sad part is, they won't find that out until after they are dead, and standing in the flames, facing the deceiver. Unless they repent and accept the Truth – Jesus is the Way, the Truth, the Life, and He is the only Way to heaven, they won't make it to heaven. You cannot get there by works, by killing a Jew or Christian, by keeping the law of the Ten Commandments. You cannot go to heaven, unless you go through the cross, and the blood of Jesus Christ, the Son of God. If you think that is harsh, take it up with the One who wrote it in the beginning. He tells the Truth. It is up to you to believe it.

There is therefore now no condemnation to them which are in Christ Jesus who walk not after the flesh, but after the Spirit. For the law of the Spirit of life in Christ Jesus has made me free from the law of sin and death. For what the law could not do, in that it was weak through the flesh, God sending His own Son in the likeness of sinful flesh, and for sin, condemned sin in the flesh: that the righteousness of the law might be fulfilled in us, who walk not after the flesh, but after the Spirit, for they that are after the flesh do mind the thing of the flesh; but they that are after the Spirit the things of the Spirit. For to be carnally minded is death; but to be spiritually minded is life and peace, because the carnal mind is enmity against God for it is not subject to the law of God, neither indeed can be. So then they that are in the flesh cannot please God. Romans 8:1-8

Are we subject to God? The word subject means, under the power and authority of another. Owing obedience or allegiance to another. The one definition that stuck to me was: a corpse intended for study, the doer of the action in conjunction with the receiver of the action. That made me think of a dead man, who has no rights in the hands of an undertaker, who is getting him ready to go to the grave. If we are truly born again, and God is our Father, are we the corpse in His hands, as He is getting us ready for our journey home to heaven?

Or are we people who say we are Christians, and still run our own lives, doing our own thing. Are we people who believe when we die, we will just walk into heaven and say, "Here I am." I think God loves us enough to make it easy for us to get to heaven, but when we say, "I DO", the responsibility falls on us to obey His word, and do what He tells us to do, instead of running our lives, and living the way we want to live. The wages of sin is death. God wrote a book telling us how to live the abundant life, in the here and now. The choice is ours, if we want to get saved, it is also our choice to obey and follow. If you don't obey and follow, the words you said at the cross means nothing. They fall at the cross, and the blood is trampled under your feet. You lie, when you say, "I DO", then walk off, do everything your own way, or half way, or any way other than what God says do.

People who can practice sin, and do not feel conviction, are not saved. People who can practice sin, say they are saved, and on their way to heaven are deceived, and are not saved. But, you can't judge anyone, you are saying. I am not judging a single soul on this earth. The Word is your judge. I can, however, inspect fruit and tell if it is rotten or not. I have had rotten fruit in my life, and I know when God pruned me, when He cut the rotten branches off, He made me sit on the sidelines, researching the reason why I walked in the valley of the shadow of death, and I learned something. Everyone is subject to the wiles of Satan. Even Jesus was tested in the wilderness. How did He pass the test? "IT IS WRITTEN." He said it to the enemy, over and over. It is written, and Jesus obeyed what was written. Someone may say, "Well, that was Jesus. He is different from us." Let me give you a hint, Jesus was born of a virgin woman, on this earth, lived, ate food, drank water, and went to the bathroom, just like us. He walked the same dirt we walk, and contrary to opinion, he didn't do a single miracle until the wedding he attended, when he turned water into wine. He only did, said, and listened to the Father, he OBEYED his Father. Have you ever considered, if you obeyed in the same manner as Jesus did, the Father would work through you and miracles could be happening through you?

Most people are not willing to admit they are wrong, are in a wilderness, have issues, strongholds, familiar spirits that plague them on a daily basis.

I knew a lady who was angry every time someone said a certain thing to her. She would blow up and lose control of her temper immediately. She would rave and rant for several minutes, then calm down and apologize to everyone for her actions. I asked her a question about how long this had been going on. She could not remember when it started, but she wished it would not continue. She had an awful headache afterwards that put her in bed many times. We prayed and I rebuked any spirit that was assigned to her or her family. She started to cry. She said, she felt like something left her. She didn't have the episodes again.

My sister-n-law, Martha, and I had dinner with a saved lady one evening, and were having a great time. We spent over an hour eating, and sharing our hearts. We were on the way back home when the lady stopped talking to us. She didn't answer any of our questions, and she didn't have anything to say about the bible. We were discussing how the Lord had been such a help in our families, and how He was saving those closest to us. We arrived at Martha's house. I was going to take the lady home. We all got out of the car at Martha's house. The lady got into the front seat, sat down and didn't speak to us again. I told Martha we would see her later, I walked around to shut the door for the lady, and noticed she was trembling all over, and her hands were gripped tightly against her side. I asked her if she was ok, but she didn't respond. I leaned down to look at her face, she began to fall over sideways, and her shaking increased. The Lord said, "She is possessed with a demon. She needs deliverance." I asked Martha to come help me get her out of the car. When we lifted her out of the car, she could not stand on her own, so we held her up by her arms, as we supported her between us. Her head rolled back, and her eyes changed from blue to gray. She had no pupils, she was foaming at the mouth. Martha and I started praying, then the Spirit of the Lord took over, and I said, "Spirit of infirmity, In Jesus name you have no authority. I bind the strongman, and every imp under its authority to remove yourself from this woman. Loose her and let her go. The blood of Jesus is covering her, and nothing can stay, harm or hold on to her. In Jesus name GO. Go to the feet of Jesus and He will deal with you this day." Suddenly she stopped shaking, she lifted her head, and her eyes cleared up and changed back to blue. She stood on her own feet and said, "What are you doing? What's wrong?" We turned her loose, and started praising the Lord she was free. We asked her what she remembered. She said, "We were eating at the restaurant, and now we are home. I don't remember coming home. I don't remember eating either. I know this, I feel like a new person. I feel wonderful. Whatever has been plaguing me, isn't now. What did you two do?" We told her what she did, and how her eyes changed. We told her about how she stop talking, and the shaking. She didn't remember any of it. She said she saw a fog standing way out in front of her when she could see again. She felt like a new person, there was joy and peace in her heart. We all rejoiced in her deliverance by the Lord. I spoke to her recently, and she said she was reading, studying her bible, learning to live by the Word, and she was doing the Word, because she was hearing the Spirit of the Lord speak to her all the time.

Where are you today? Ask yourself this question; do I want the Lord to control every aspect of my life? Am I willing to obey every word I read in the Bible, and do it? Am I willing to obey every word I hear the Spirit of the Lord speak to my heart and Do IT? What about eating right? Giving of your time and money? Speaking to someone you think little of, doing a good deed for someone you do not like, or just taking the time to call on people who need a hand or listening ear? What about exercising to lose some weight? What about

This is my prayer: will you pray it with me?

Lord, into your hands do I submit my body, soul and spirit. I relinquish control of my life to your Son and ask you to deliver me from all things displeasing to you. Make my life, a life that counts and is the image of your Son who died for me. I give you my decision making, and ask for Your will to be done in, and through me from this day forward. Let the light of Your Word be so impressed on my soul, that my soul lines up with YOUR Spirit, and my body becomes your temple on earth, as in heaven, filled with your glory. In Jesus name, amen.

Friends, family and those who love the LORD, I say; RECEIVE THE EAR and OBEY!

To the rest of you, what are you waiting for?

Jesus is coming soon, whether you believe it or not!

Notes: All scripture is from the King James Bible

Quotes from Hal Lindsey's book - Satan is Alive and Living on Planet Earth by Hal Lindsey –This book brought me to salvation.

Word meanings:

American Heritage Dictionary

Hebrew/Greek Strong's Concordance

This book was written to give you something to think about. Ask questions and research for answers. Study your Bible to show yourself approved unto God.

About the Author:

I write to allow the Spirit to teach me and others, what it means to listen. I write to grow in grace and understanding. I write to share my heart with others. If you agree, that is ok. If you don't agree, that is ok.

I would like everyone to study the word, listen to the Spirit, and see what is going on around you and in this world. I believe Jesus is coming soon. All the things going on around the world make me tremble. I know He has everything under control, but I also know people are not ready.

I pray eyes will be opened to see, ears will open to hear and hearts will be renewed before the trump of God is blown and the dead in Christ rise, and we that remain shall be changed in the twinkling of an eye.

To contact this author:

PO BOX 1847

Powder Springs, Ga. 30127

Other Books:

Revelation To Me
Journey Home – Lost to Found
Brady - Book One
David - Book Two
Short Stories: Ronny's Story
　　　　　　　Caleb's Story
　　　　　　　Hope's Story

Made in the USA
Charleston, SC
01 December 2014